ZEPPELIN HUNTERS

SIMON CHAPMAN

Badger Publishing Limited
Oldmedow Road,
Hardwick Industrial Estate,
King's Lynn PE30 4JJ
Telephone: 01438 791037

www.badgerlearning.co.uk

8 10 9

Zeppelin Hunters ISBN 978-1-78147-555-3

Text © Simon Chapman 2014
Complete work © Badger Publishing Limited 2014

All rights reserved. No part of this publication may be reproduced, stored in any form or by any means mechanical, electronic, recording or otherwise without the prior permission of the publisher.

The right of Simon Chapman to be identified as author of this work has been asserted by him in accordance with the Copyright, Designs and Patents Act 1988.

Publisher: Susan Ross
Senior Editor: Danny Pearson
Designer: Fiona Grant

Photos: Cover image: /AP/Press Association Images
Page 5: Universal History Archive/UN/REX
Page 7: Daily Mail /REX
Page 12: The Royal Navy
Page 13: JACQUES BRINON/AP/Press Association Images
Page 14: CSU Archives/Everett Collect/REX
Page 17: Courtesy Everett Collection/REX
Page 19: Max Smith
Page 22: Juliet Breese
Page 25: Juliet Breese
Page 26: Juliet Breese
Page 28: Sipa Press/REX
Page 29: David Sandison/The Independent/REX
Page 30: Jae C. Hong/AP/Press Association Images
Page 31: WestEnd61/REX

Attempts to contact all copyright holders have been made.
If any omitted would care to contact Badger Learning, we will be happy to make appropriate arrangements.

ZEPPELIN HUNTERS

Contents

1.	World War One	4
2.	What is a Zeppelin?	6
3.	How to destroy a Zeppelin	9
4.	Reggie Warneford	12
5.	The Home Front	16
6.	William Leefe Robinson	18
7.	The end of Zeppelin raids	27
8.	Airships today	29
	Index	32

Badger LEARNING

1. WORLD WAR ONE

German Zeppelins were dropping bombs on Britain and there was nothing anyone could do about it.

These lighter-than-air 'ships of the sky' flew higher than any plane could reach and they came at night, often hidden in the clouds.

They could not be seen. They could not be shot down.

People from Edinburgh down to London were terrified. The Zeppelin menace had to be stopped.

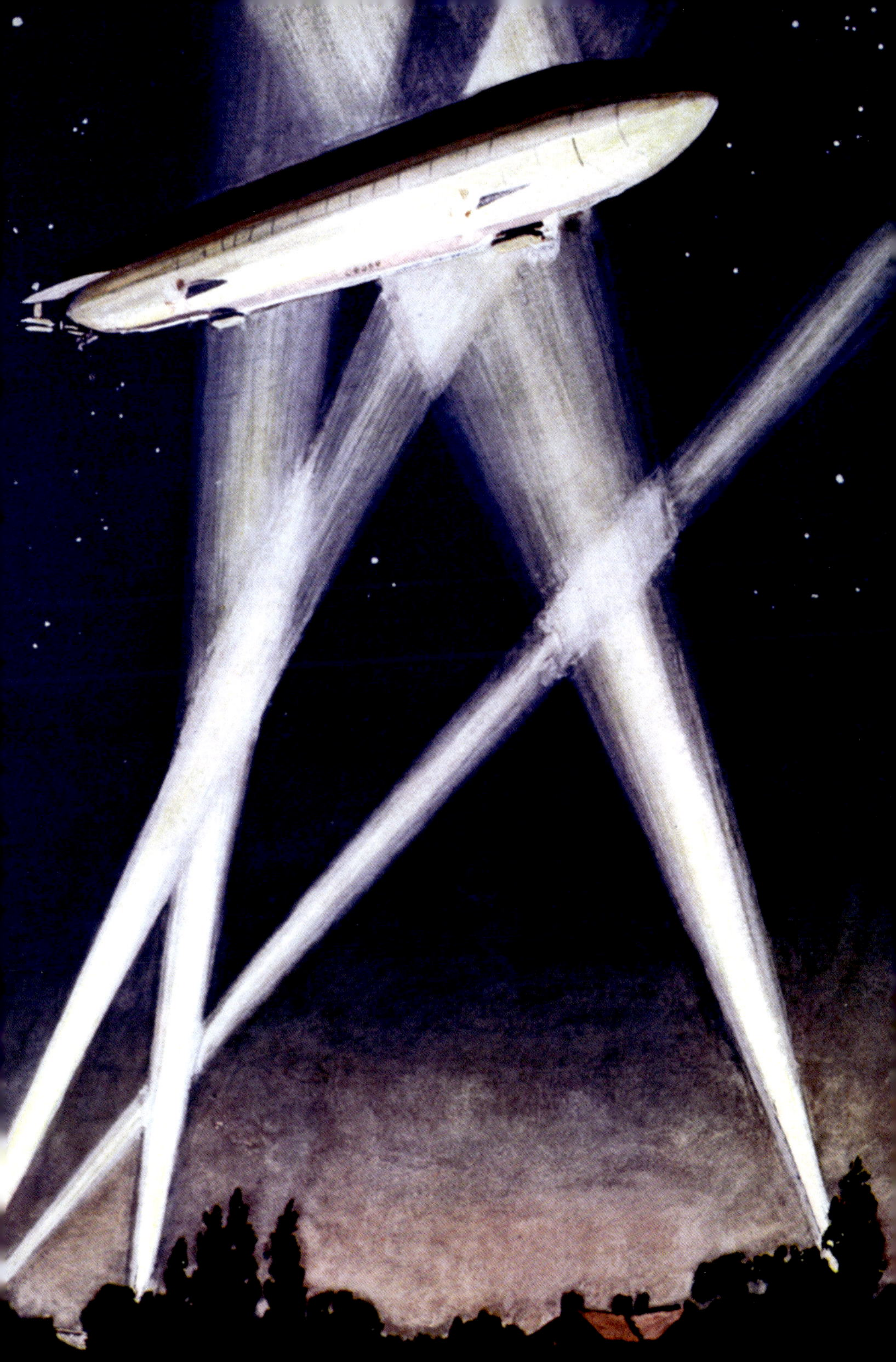

2. WHAT IS A ZEPPELIN?

FAST FACTS

1916 M Class Zeppelin L31

Length: 200m

Construction: Aluminium framework filled with hydrogen bags; cloth outer skin; 3 propeller engines

Speed: 50mph

Operating altitude: 4,000m

Armament: Up to 9 machine guns mounted on top and in the cupolas underneath; 4,000kg of bombs

These giant airships were filled with hydrogen gas, which is explosive, so getting rid of them should have been easy. All the pilots of the Royal Naval Air Service needed was a way of setting fire to that gas.

At 3,600 metres altitude.

At night.

But in 1915, when the Zeppelins started coming, hardly anyone had tried flying at night and very few planes were equipped with guns.

Zeppelins weren't only used for bombing – they were also used to spy on the enemy.

A 'sub-cloud car' was a one-man capsule that could be lowered 1,500 metres.

The Zeppelin could stay hidden in a cloud while the observer telephoned up enemy positions.

3. HOW TO DESTROY A ZEPPELIN

The British commanders said the solution to the problem was obvious. Attack the airships in the daytime – drop bombs on them. However, that was a lot easier to say than do!

First, the pilots had to fly above the airship, which was hard to do without being seen.

Then they had to accurately drop an explosive that would hit the airship.

Finally, even if they managed all that, there was no guarantee that the bomb would puncture the grey cloth outer skin of the airship and ignite the hydrogen gas bags inside.

Various ideas were tried out:
- hand grenades dangled on long lines
- bombs with grapple hooks that would catch on the cloth
- explosive ammunition

Everyone liked the last idea best. It was the only one where the plane didn't have to fly above the Zeppelin. That meant they didn't have to face the deadly fire of up to nine machine guns at close range.

The trouble was, someone would have to invent explosive bullets and someone else would have to work out how to fit machine guns to the flimsy planes.

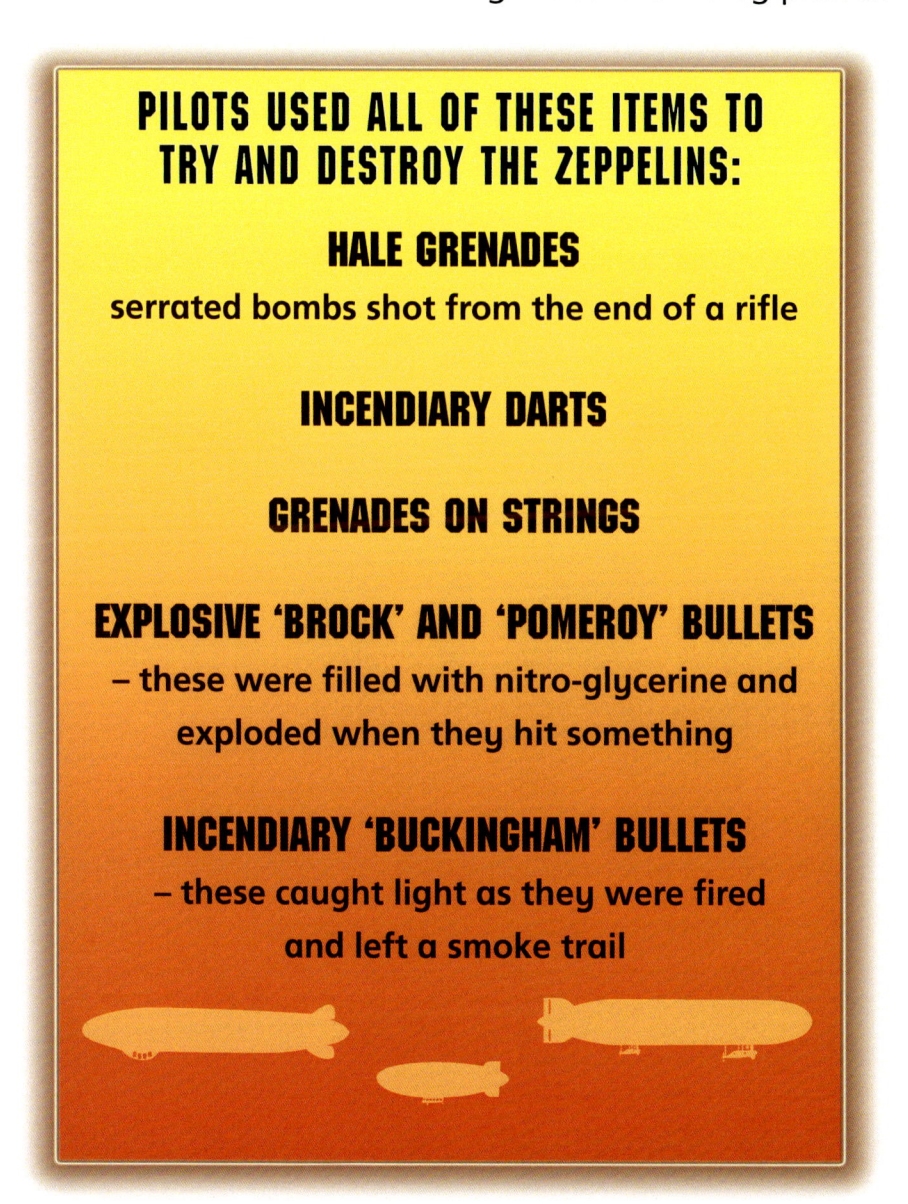

PILOTS USED ALL OF THESE ITEMS TO TRY AND DESTROY THE ZEPPELINS:

HALE GRENADES
serrated bombs shot from the end of a rifle

INCENDIARY DARTS

GRENADES ON STRINGS

EXPLOSIVE 'BROCK' AND 'POMEROY' BULLETS
– these were filled with nitro-glycerine and exploded when they hit something

INCENDIARY 'BUCKINGHAM' BULLETS
– these caught light as they were fired and left a smoke trail

4. REGGIE WARNEFORD

A pilot called Reggie Warneford was about to show that the Zeppelins were not invincible.

Reggie was flying a mission to find out where the Zeppelins were based. His plane, a Morane L Monoplane, was very light and quite fast compared to others of the day (78mph).

The Morane was unarmed, except for six bombs and a short-barrelled rifle that Reggie kept in an old boot in the cockpit.

1915 Morane L Monoplane

WOW! facts

Speed: 78mph
Weapons: 6 bombs in a rack by the cockpit

Reggie was somewhere over Belgium when he saw a Zeppelin going down, perhaps to land.

The top of the Zeppelin was about as long as a football pitch – Reggie could have landed his plane on it!

Reggie flew from the rear of the Zeppelin to the nose, releasing his six bombs as he flew. He had just reached the front of the Zeppelin when the first bomb exploded.

A huge fireball rippled up the cigar-shaped body of the Zeppelin. The blast from the explosion sent Reggie's tiny monoplane tumbling end over end.

The airship was going down, but Reggie was in a dive with oil pouring out of his engine. Somehow, amazingly, he landed the Morane in a field. He knew he was behind German lines so he prepared to burn his plane. But no German soldiers turned up.

Reggie had a look at the plane's engine and found the pipe where the oil had been leaking. Reggie had a cigarette holder of about the same size as the broken oil line, so he used that as a replacement. Reggie fixed the engine and flew back to the British lines in time for tea!

Reggie was the first to shoot down a Zeppelin in World War One. He was awarded the Victoria Cross for his action.

As for the Zeppelin – unfortunately it hit a convent and killed two nuns. All but one of its crew of 11 died.

5. THE HOME FRONT

Zeppelin raids were causing more and more damage on the Home Front. Reggie Warneford had shown that it was possible to destroy the airships if they were close to the ground. However, once they were high in the air, Zeppelins were still virtually impossible to catch.

Air raid damage in London during the First World War

The Germans moved their bases back from the front line and carried on the raids. It could be said that most of the attacks did little damage when compared with the Second World War bombing raids. However, the menace of the Zeppelins was the terror they caused. The British people's morale was slipping.

By September 1916, planes were ready with a mixture of explosive and incendiary (bullets that cause fires) ammunition in their machine guns. And, just as important, pilots had been trained to fly in the dark.

6. WILLIAM LEEFE ROBINSON

On the night of 2nd September 1916, sixteen Zeppelins headed out to bomb London. William Leefe Robinson in his BE2c Night Fighter set off on the 3,600 metre climb to reach the airships.

The climb to that altitude would take 53 minutes. William's plane had an upwards-slanting Lewis machine gun armed with the new ammunition.

1916 BE2c Night Fighter

WOW! facts

Speed: 72mph
Weapons: 45 degree upward-facing Lewis machine gun armed with a mixture of incendiary (flaming) and explosive ammunition

Just getting close to the airship was dangerous.

William was afraid of attracting fire from the Zeppelin's machine guns, as well as 'friendly fire' from the ground.

Searchlights panned the sky and flak guns shot at anything caught in their beam.

The flak guns' shells exploded in mid-air and sent lethal shrapnel through any airship – or aeroplane – nearby.

William swooped in and machine-gunned the huge airship.

One ammunition drum was gone.

No effect.

Maybe the new ammunition did not work. William eased off the throttle and hid in a cloud while he clipped on another drum of bullets.

He attacked again.

Nothing.

The bullets just passed straight through the airship's skin.

He reloaded again.

This time he came in really close, concentrating all his fire on just one spot on the underside of the Zeppelin.

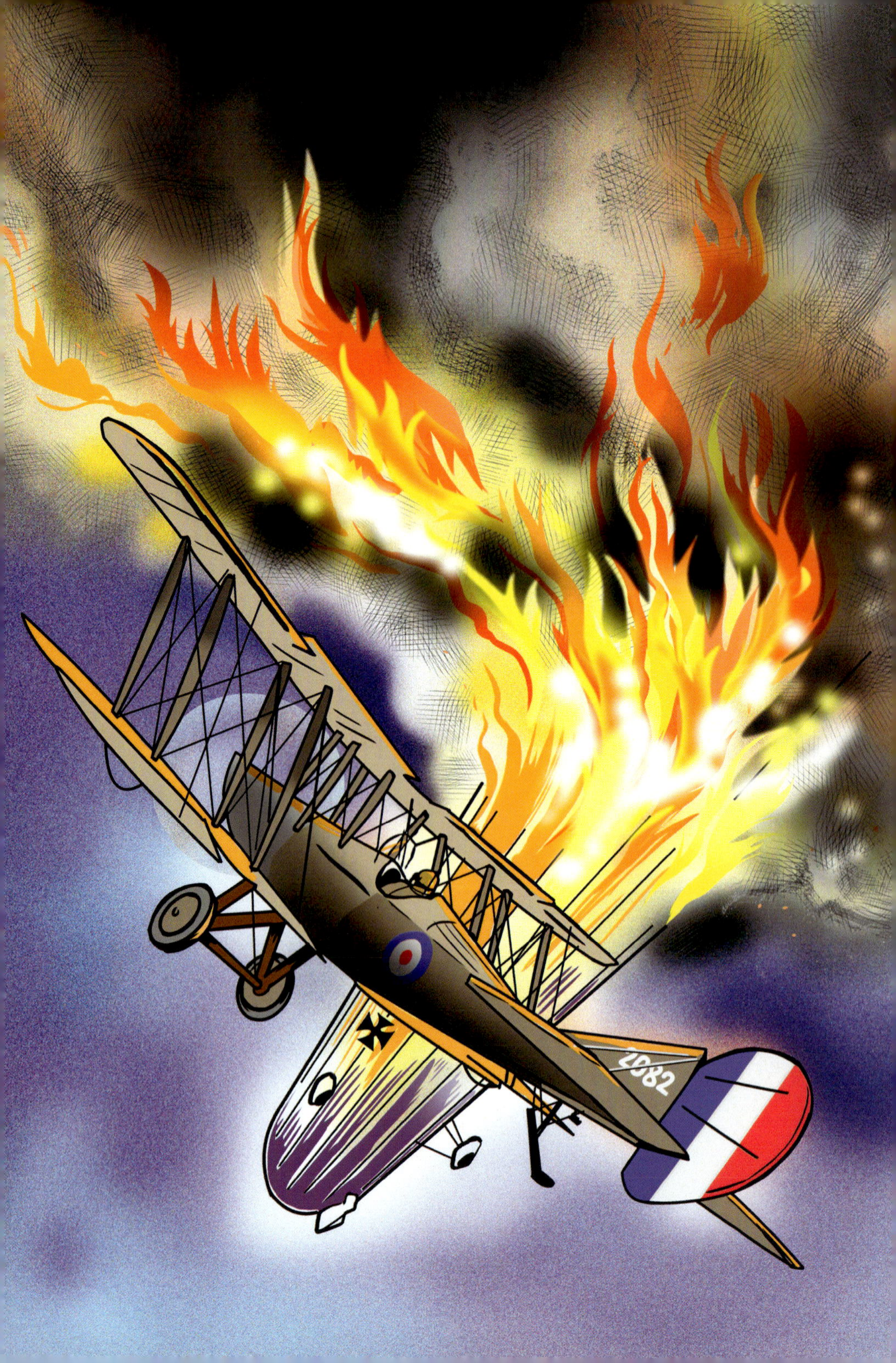

Suddenly, inside the grey cigar shape, a red glow grew and burst outwards. The rear half of the Zeppelin was on fire. For a second it hung in the air. Then it went down.

Below, in the London district of Woolwich, people were celebrating. They had watched everything. Now they were dancing and singing. One man even brought out a set of bagpipes and started playing them.

William returned to ground a hero. Like Reggie Warneford, he too was awarded the Victoria Cross. He also won £3,500 in cash prizes.

The Victoria Cross

Newspaper headline when William Leefe Robinson was awarded the Victoria Cross

Zeppelin v. plane

1917 Sopwith Camel 'Comic'

WOW! facts

Speed: 115mph
Weapons: 2 Lewis machine guns on top of the wings with explosive ammunition (The machine guns were originally in the 'nose' but these were moved as the flashes when they fired ruined the pilots' night vision.)

1917 Supermarine Nighthawk

WOW! facts

Speed: 75mph
Weapons: 2 Lewis machine guns, a 37mm cannon, a searchlight in the nose powered by a petrol generator. This four-winged beast of a plane had a crew of five and was intended to stay in the air for between 9 and 18 hours. But it was too slow to catch up with the Zeppelins and only one was ever built.

7. THE END OF ZEPPELIN RAIDS

With explosive and incendiary ammunition, the British had shown they could shoot down Zeppelins. Over the next few months, four more were shot down by British night fighters. For a while the Germans tried flying at higher altitudes to avoid the biplanes. However, lack of oxygen made the crews weak and forgetful, and the intense cold weakened the airships' structure.

Too few Zeppelins were making it back after each raid. Though the Germans continued night bombing with long-range biplanes, the Zeppelin menace was over.

THE END OF THE "BABY-KILLER".

Like many pilots in World War One, both William Leefe Robinson and Reggie Warneford died young.

William was wounded and died when he was just 23 from Spanish Flu. Reggie was killed in an aircraft accident only 10 days after bombing the Zeppelin. He was also 23.

8. AIRSHIPS TODAY

Airships can still be seen in the skies today, although they are used for different purposes than during World War One.

Airships are often spotted flying over outdoor sporting events. They can be used to capture excellent aerial footage of these events as they are steady and quiet, making them perfect for the job.

The Aeroscraft is a prototype airship with a very large cargo bay. It can be loaded and unloaded hovering above the ground.

It can also take off and land vertically, making it an excellent vehicle for delivering food and other emergency supplies to disaster areas and war zones.

If this airship successfully goes into production, it will be a more environmentally friendly and low-cost solution to our transport needs than the planes in use now.

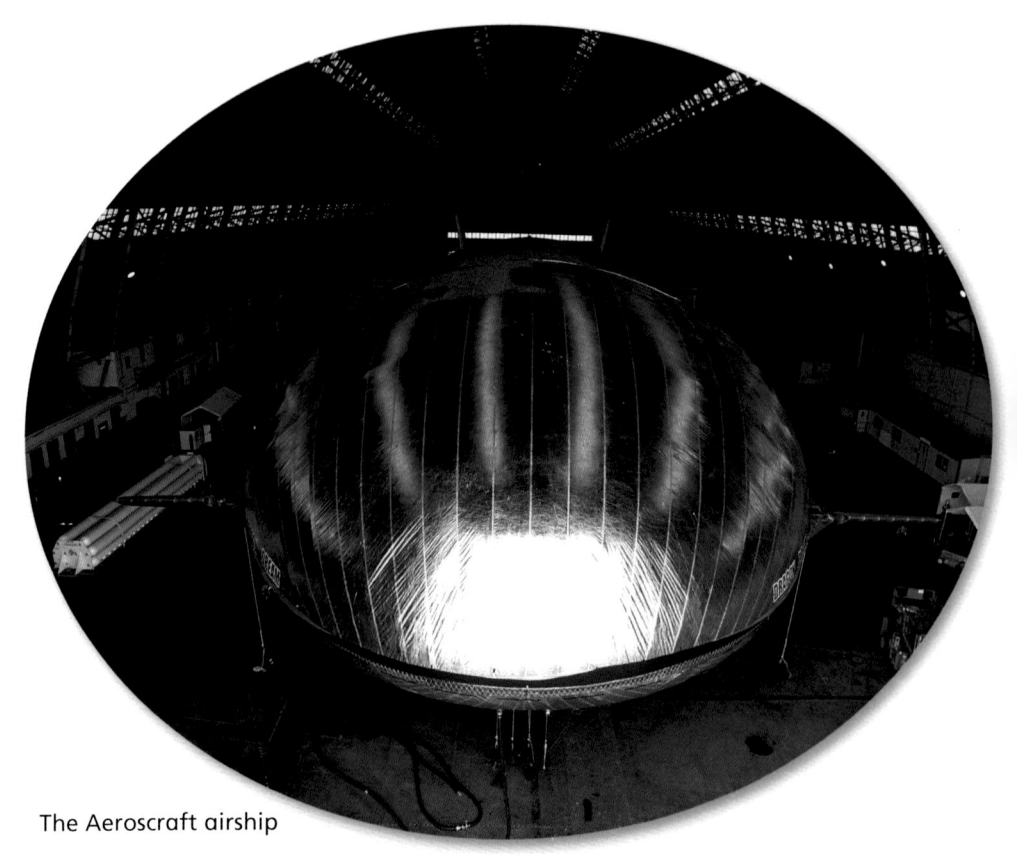

The Aeroscraft airship

Who knows what the future will hold for the airship.

The sky's the limit!

INDEX

Aeroscraft, the 30
airships 7, 9, 16, 18, 27, 29-31
altitude 6, 7, 18, 27
ammunition 10, 17, 18, 19, 21, 25, 27
BE2c Night Fighter 18-19
bombs 4, 6, 9, 10, 12, 13, 14
British 9, 15, 17, 27
bullets 11, 17, 21
enemy 8
explosive 7, 9, 10, 11, 17, 19, 25, 27
friendly fire 20
Germans 17, 27
grenades 10, 11
guns 7, 20
Home Front, the 16-17
hydrogen 6, 7, 9
incendiary 11, 17, 19, 27
machine guns 6, 10, 11, 17, 20, 25, 26
Morane L Monoplane 12-13
pilots 7, 9, 11, 17, 25, 28
planes 7, 11, 17, 30
Robinson, William Leefe 18-24, 28
Royal Naval Air Service 7
searchlights 20
Sopwith Camel 'Comic' 25
speed 6, 13, 19, 25, 26
sub-cloud car 8
Supermarine Nighthawk 26
Victoria Cross 15, 23, 24
Warneford, Reggie 12-15, 16, 23, 28
weapons 13, 19, 25, 26
World War One 4, 15, 28